Blue

Moon

88 POEMS

SHARAN CHEEMA

This book is dedicated to
my daughter, Amar.

CONTENTS

Soul Connection

I

MY FIRST LOVE

My first intoxication
My first wish
My first dream
My first hope

    The skipping of my heartbeats

My eyes have fallen into yours, right from the start
The mischief in your voice melts the heaviness in my heart

As my eyes sway and dance in your eyes
My soul is flying through the bright blue skies

I will wait lifetimes
        upon lifetimes
            upon lifetimes
                for your love

You were made for me before the planets and the Stars up
    above

My first, pure, true love

MY GOOD TIME SPIRIT

Come lift me up, let us fly together
You are my good time spirit
I have wanted you, for me, always
After losing you, my heart has become weak

My floating soul will always come back to you
Come, make my heartbeat strong again
Your name is upon my lips
In my mind is your picture in a frame
You have made me yours and I can begin to wish for love again

After knowing you, my heart yearns for you
How do they who cannot love, live their lives
They live with stones in their hearts
From you I will never part

My beautiful goodtime spirit

FLOATING SOULS

My eyes do not rest
My nights are sleepless
My soul is floating North, East, South and West
My life is worthless

Only a floating soul understands the pain of love
Only a floating soul seeks the meaning of life
When your eyes met with mine
I saw the Sunshine and the Moonlight
I saw the magic of love; I saw the Stars shining bright

Your loving ways taught me the poetry of the seasons
Your eyes intoxicated me, and my lips became still
Come show my floating soul the magic of love again

MY YEARNING NIRVANA

When we first met, we were young and free
With nothing to lose
We had the Universe at our feet

I kept my memories of you safe in my heart
Then my soul guided me back to you
When the Starlight of your eyes
Shone into the darkness of my soul
You reminded me that you were my yearning nirvana

You are a waterfall of love overflowing in my heart
This love has poured out all over my world
You have set the ocean of my heart on fire

I want to shout to every Universe
That I have found my
                soul connection
                    my twin flame
                        my yearning nirvana

PLANET OF LOVE

Fly me far away from the Moon's Stars
Let us transcend further than Earth, Venus, Saturn, and Mars

Let us fly higher
    and let our love run deeper
        until we both feel the edge of the Cosmos

My Soul Connection
My Twin Flame
My Yearning Nirvana

        Let us float together through the galaxies and milky ways
            forever

We can find a planet made just for us
With our own Moonshine and cosmic dust
Where we can sit under the waterfalls
And our dreams can come alive
Higher past the Sunsets in the Earth's blue skies

Where our floating souls can intertwine
Where we can weave our spirits together as one
Where we can breathe and reach enlightenment together on
    this magical journey

What shall we name our planet of love?

TWIN FLAMES

Our souls parted a million years ago
Then your soul touched my soul on Earth briefly
Your spirit as pure as liquid gold
My heart as soft as silk

Once again,
   we parted
      suddenly
         and without words

For years to come our souls were circling the Universe
Searching for each other

Until finally one day, my soul returned home to you again
You opened the doors to your heart and let me in
Where I could roam freely and without shame
Our souls had reconnected from deep within

The rains poured for days and nights
Years of pain and hurt endured in your absence my whole life

I turned to face my heart's truth
As I felt my love for you bloom
You smoothed out all my imperfections,
               with your every passion
Whilst I talked to my Moon

A love with no name
That cannot be measured by time, space nor distance
Our spirits must intertwine and awaken each other

MEMORIES OF YOU

The first day I looked into your eyes
I saw shooting Stars across the skies

You came back and showed my body and soul
The meaning of desire
You brought my missing heartbeats back to make me whole
You set my spirit on fire

You filled me with both pleasure and pain all at once
You filled me with fire and rain all at once

My body has become like hot and dry sand
Come quench my thirst
Fill me with that beautiful fire and rain, please understand
Come for me now, but please do not hurt

Love

II

A STORM OF LOVE

A love storm is brewing
The gentle breeze is growing stronger
Whilst your spirit surrounds me

When the soft winds blow sweetly
I feel the love in the air
                    caressing my hair

 In every moment
        I feel your heartbeat upon my lips
                        we can only imagine this

                I am falling all over the thought of you

Watch your footsteps because I cannot control my eyes
Watch your eyes because I cannot control my heart

A storm of love is coming over us...

A STORM OF STARS

All my heart's pains are smiling
       seeing you again
Joyous like a dancing storm of Stars
       are these pains
All the love and memories come flooding back right from the
   start
       again; all over again

Your touch and your silence re-ignite the fire in my heart
Your electricity is running
         deep through my veins

My passion comes alive
       for a love that has been hidden for years
I cannot breathe as I am lost in time
      a lifetime of longing is finally over
       I have nothing to fear

The world is silent…

I am melting
     into you
Whilst you are
     falling
      all over me

Let the Stars rain down a storm tonight
Let this moment last forever
        until it is all over again

LOVE IS IN THE AIR

We re-connected and our love for each other
Began to blow softly through the wind
Without us both realising
Preparing to create a storm in the air, without a care

This storm of love was preparing to set fire to my soul

Love proceeded to move in unison with the Stars in the sky
My sweetest dreams scattered amongst the Stars up high
Will these dreams ever become a reality for my heart
We loved each other truly from the start
Only to be pulled apart

Which way do I turn?
How do I call his name?
How do I find him when I awake from my dreams?

YOU ARE...

My free-spirited butterfly
My beauty of a rose
My good time spirit
My yearning nirvana
My floating soul
My fragrance of a summer meadow
My springtime daffodil
My nothing and my everything
My heartbeat
My spirit and my soul
The Sun of my life
My every smile
My true pure love
My surety
My shining Star
My unquenchable thirst

The breath of my first love

MY FIRST WISH, MY
LAST DREAM

I long for your touch
Every wound of my heart has been blessed by you
I can no longer call out for your love

You were my first wish
You will be my last dream

DEAR HEART

Today I have understood his eyes
I have found my love
Dear heart, do not stop beating
I am worthy of his love

I agree to all your requests
My every gaze will smile forever
I have found my love, he has found his life
I am his love, he is my life

Tell the world I have found my love
His cool shadows have fallen onto my fiery soul
I hear the sweet music of love everywhere

DEEPER INTO YOU

(Woman)

My eyes move towards you
Oh beloved, break away from your fears
My eyes move deeper into you

I have become crazy for you
Though you will never realise my worth
My eyes move deeper into you

Why when I am close to you, do I give you my love?
When I give you my love, I am full of regret
My heart is raw
I move deeper into you

(Man)

What do you know my innocent love
How can I live the burden of life
I carry a heavy load
My eyes move deeper into you

Softly, softly my tears fall from my soul
My heart hurts with your heart
My eyes move deeper into you

INTOXICATED

Into my lover's eyes I am falling deeply
I have become intoxicated
My guilty pleasure is my intoxication
I am content in this guilty pleasure

I have no fear when staring deeply into your eyes
You have made me courageous in becoming intoxicated
With the reluctant acceptance of your eyes, I am intoxicated

In the floating clouds, your name resounds and surrounds me
Your sweet soul becomes my fragrance
As the sweet love in the air blows gently through my hair
I come back down to earth and again your eyes intoxicate me

My love for you, my longing for you
The love drug in your eyes has made me lose myself in you
You have intoxicated me

Whether you are near or far
You will always remain in my heart
I am a dimming flame on a cold dark night
You warm me up and reignite me so I can shine brightly

I am intoxicated

GAZING EYES

Seeing you again
    I stop suddenly in my footsteps
        gazing, gazing, gazing
           smiling to myself coyly

I am left speechless
    my lips are silenced
I am transcended
    so lost in your eyes

These long nights are a lonely journey
I dream and wish for my beloved to be close to me
    lost, lost, lost

Seeing you I blush; I see the reflection of my pain in your eyes
    Into your deep brown eyes
        I have fallen

In my dreams I look to find you
In the winding paths of your eyes, I am a prisoner
I search for my journey of happiness
Whilst my soul smiles, as I am gazing into your eyes

UPON OUR LIPS

Upon your lips
    I wish I might beautifully place my lips

Come let us fly high so I can sing softly to you
Should I stumble over your salty sea tears
I shall turn them into the silver of the Moon

I am tired of remembering you
          and remembering you
             and remembering you
I wish you would remember me
                  just once

The dark night sky is above us both, missing its Moon and Stars
The Sun wishes to light up the sky with its very own fire

As my mind has its final hiccup
Even death sings a poem of its own

Upon your lips
    I wish I might beautifully place my lips

Come let us fly high so I can sing softly to you

UNDERNEATH THE STARS

For we might never meet again in this Moonlight
Hold me underneath the shining Stars
Destiny has brought us back together this night
Where you no longer look at me from afar

It is a promise that I will not return to your arms
time and time again
once this night has passed

Hold me underneath the Stars
Or else the rains will pour from my eyes and flood my soul
after this painful goodbye

Hold me so close
that our souls can physically intertwine
Come close, embrace me

Feel the beat of my heart and let your heart
Beat with mine

EVERLASTING LOVE SONG

May I kiss your sweet lips
Then you hold my head in your chest?
Will you make my love song everlasting?
We are tied in our dreams
And in the hearts and souls of lovers

May we make new dreams together
Where the Universe does not make a sound
Where I only hear your love
Will you make my love song everlasting?

ONLY FOR YOU

Honestly…I am not crazy
I am only crazy for you
I am just so alone and so in love all at the same time
I love with my heart on my sleeve

My spirit yearns my soulmate once more
I feel every emotion to its core

I wish this feeling would pass
Only I can turn love into hate
When will you tell me to forget you and end things fast?
When will our love end and when will my heart break?

DAYDREAM

You take my hand and hold it tight
I feel so loved, it just feels right
But what I long for in my heart of pain
Is when you will hold me in your arms again

You pull me near; you hold me close
I hear your heartbeat and only God knows
This is pure, this is love
I do not want this to end, please do not ever let me go

JOURNEY OF LIFE

How do I travel with you on the journey of life, my beloved
You are the depth of the ocean, I am the sweet air breeze
You take me away with my hand in your hand

With the soft sound of your footsteps
        the doors of my heart open
            and I am crazy for you

You are the fragrance of a spring evening
I am your shining Star
You are the surety of my life, and you hold me up
From all of God's creations, I have chosen you
You are the depth of the ocean, I am the sweet air breeze

The way you move, the stars also proceed to move
Like the tears of my soul
Dreams of dreams burn my eyes
Like desires of my dreams
Your destination is my path

You are the depth of the ocean
I am the sweet air breeze
How do I travel with you on the journey of my life, my beloved

Passion

III

IGNITE MY PASSION

Hold me tight and hold me forever
Let me burn the tears in your eyes
I crave your love of life in every weather
Take me with you on your magical ride

The sweet fragrance of your spirit encapsulates me
What is a heart?
I will give you my life and soul freely

Ignite this passion in my heart with your fire
Oh beloved, quench this thirst in my eyes
With your heart's desire
Let us set the Sun on fire
Let us make our Moon blush and smile

DESIRES OF THE HEART

Do not hide away from me today
Set your eyes on me
Make me rich in your love I pray
Do not deny me your beauty

Let us embrace each other
Listen to my heart's desires
        and share your heart's desires with me
My heart has drank all my blood dry
I have cried and all my tears have dried up

I have counted all the Stars in the sky
Till they can no longer be seen
Why do the Stars no longer revolve around Venus

Come to me my beloved
Fulfil my desires I pray
I wait for you to return to me
Whilst my candle burns an eternal flame

Come put this burning flame out with your love

Let our eyes meet one more time
Before we disappear back into the Universe

Can we satisfy our souls and spirits for a moment of love?

MY HEART'S DESIRE

Your eyes and your smile are my heart's desire
They have caught me and seduced me in a single glance

I am hooked onto your spirit
       hook me onto your body
              and I shall hold you tightly, forever
Do not let this moment be over
              this feeling of being together

I have fantasised about this moment
       take a moment to understand
Now it seems we are here
Touch every part of me
       with your lips, skin, and hands

Say you want nobody else, only me, make it clear
Make my fire burn stronger for you
Let this moment last forever
I am all emptied out
Come fill me up, let us fulfil our heart's desires together

ROSES AND THORNS

Your lips are rosy, red, fragrant, and delicate
Like the soft, sultry, summer rose
How I long to press my lips upon yours
Until the winter frost grows
When our lips might have frozen together, forever

Your soft warm breath on my skin
Your arms embrace me with your strength
Until I feel every breath within my body
Is this love or is this a sin?

Then I feel those sharp thorns
I have always seen the sparkle of anger in your eyes
So, it comes with no surprise
Those thorns I have felt them, oh so many times

This rose teases my soft heart
Its thorns will cut my skin and bleed out my love

Once upon a time
    in a land far, far away
        I will wake up in a garden of dreams and roses
        and live happily ever after

MOMENTS OF LOVE

Those moments we shared
Those words we exchanged
Those nights
Those memories that lit flames
Then the rains poured, and it stormed for days and days

You will never know, and I will never know
Which season we were in and where the soft music came from

How my sadness made the Sun blush
How the Moon had missed the Sun
Since the beginning of time and for all the years to come

Our love grew deeper
The soft winds caressed and comforted me
Where did those winds come from?
Did those winds reach you before we had to part again?

ALWAYS ON MY MIND

Listen to my heart and I will feel you too
Come before me, so I see only you
Hold me in your arms
    so, I can become yours and you can become mine
Oh beautiful love
    let me steal you from the Universe, for the rest of time
It is always you
    you are always on my mind

COME FOR ME

Beautiful lover
Come for me

In the still of the night
Come for me

In the storm of the night
Understand what is stolen in my heart

To my beating heart, the melodies of your spirit will bring
    a passionate love
Come let us bring our hearts and souls together
    so we can become one

Let my cool lips touch your hot skin

Come…

SPIRIT AND SOUL

I am
   hungry for your spirit
You are
   thirsty for my soul

My fears are
   lost in your spirit
Your heart is
   lost in my soul

Your spirit
   beckons me
And my soul
   surrounds you

You give me strength so I can make you
   feel my love all around you

Your happiness gives me the strength to smile

Bring the passion of your sweet spirit into my body
And enlighten my soul, softly

A BEAUTIFUL DREAM

I have been woken up by a beautiful dream

In my dream my soul belongs to you
Just as the bright Stars belong to the Moon
And the Moon belongs to the Sun

My body is restless and craves only you in my dreams
Take me higher to Venus so we can experience pure bliss

In my dreams I can see Stars across the skies of your eyes
The Moon fades away as a new day begins

I have been woken up by a beautiful dream

I fall in love the way you fall asleep
You stir up my soul and my spirit
The Moon fades away as a new day begins

I have been woken up by a beautiful dream

STARDUST IN YOUR EYES

When I look into your eyes, I see magical Stardust
Your Starlight draws me into you
I wish I could draw you into me, so you trust in me
To love you wholeheartedly

When I look into your eyes
I see the sweetness of a fragrant red rose,
But this is not how the story goes…

You held out your hand of friendship to me
You made me a promise you would keep

I told my heart
            this promise will not be kept
I knew you would leave and go far away
And so my heart wept

When you are out of sight
My heart becomes heavy and weighs me down
An image of beauty which sets you apart, is your light
You light up the dark night sky, with your Stardust eyes, light brown

Stay with me and let me gaze into your eyes forever
You are the love of my heart
Oh, the pain when you steal a glance at me!
When our eyes lock together…
Like they did at the beginning

Do not hide away now
I can console my heart later
It already knows my pain
Show me the Stardust and the promises
In your eyes again

UNTIL FOREVER

Upon my breath…
    Until forever…
I feel the fragrances of your words within my soul

I still hear the music of those days
I saw every emotion in the glass of your eyes
In so many ways

Each time you come closer to me
Then disappear under the light of the Moon
You are still on my mind, in my dreams
When I awake you come closer again, I long to see you soon

The love that shines from our hearts daily
    has become our song
Our songs sing like the diamond Stars of our Universe
    as they dance along

The butterfly flutters of my heart are enchanted
By the excitement in your eyes
Come fulfil my desires
Embrace me in your fires

Missing You

IV

SUNSET OF LOVE

As the Sun begins to set on this summer's evening
I start to go
           crazy, crazy, crazy for you
I will miss you
           deeply, deeply, deeply on this Starry night ahead

Those beautiful moments that have passed
Those painful regrets which meant our love could not last
Those loving words on your lips
That one night of us, which slipped
           away, away, away

The cool breeze blows
My body and my soul are on fire
Please do not tease my heart this night, as only God knows
It feels so empty, yet so heavy, my soul is tired

Every season steals my heart in the night
The birds sing their last song of the evening, then home they fly
When will you quench this thirst of mine?
Will you come for me tonight?

MY HEART AWAITS YOURS

How do I explain to you, love of my life
My mind does not settle without you
You do not see how deep this love is of mine
This love which awaits your touch, is so pure and true

You have lived in my heart
Yet you do not see my heart's pain or love
Without you my heart cries alone
My heart can only live, die and be born again with you inside

Come to me, each breath of mine awaits your fragrance
Without you, how can I make my sadness disappear far away
There is only love in the veins of my heart
There is only truth in the pains of my soul

Come, hold me in your arms forever

A SUMMER THOUGHT

When I saw you on this summer day
    a thought came to my mind
That you are like the rays of the sweet, hot Sun in the sky
Today my heart made a request to my soul
Today I cooled my heart in the soft warm breeze

My heavy heart beating, my breath stuck like a lump in my
    throat
When you leave me again today
I will think about what I have given away
I will long for what you have stolen away

When I saw you on this summer day
    a thought came to my mind
Why does time sing this love song?

THOSE DAYS

Secretly I cry tears through the night
Remembering the days I fell in love with you
Those days where I could be my own self
I still remember the way you looked into my eyes
Whenever we met

I remember the colours of your love washing over me
In those sunny days when we were so young
Today the pains of the rain wash over me

Secretly, I wish to meet you in our quiet place
As I remember the days
When our hearts first met

We promised each other, we are friends for life
Secretly I cry tears through the night
Remembering the days I fell in love with you

Pain and

Sadness

V

THAT LOVE

That love that you and I had
Do you remember?
That promise you made to me
Do you recall?

After inhaling your love drug, my sadness overwhelms me

The Moonlight pinches me
    along with the attacking light of the stars
The sharpness of your laughter stabs me from afar

Your love drug is on my lips and makes me
    silently mad
I wish the Moon and the Stars would melt away, as I have become
    so sad

ONCE UPON A TIME

Once Upon a time, I could use each breath for you
Once Upon a time, I was able to devote my love and life to you
This is no longer something I can do

Words of love are being spoken again
The nights frustrate me again
This night of storms leads me astray
Tell me why is your name on my lips?
I am lost in you night and day

Remembering the beautiful times we had
I miss those times; I feel so sad

Now we are separated by distance and cannot turn back time
Come let our souls re-align

PATIENCE

I quietly await news of your love
You are patient like the tides of the waves
Your eyes so serious
The marks of your eyes have scarred me
And have taught me your brave ways

The night Moon and Stars belong to you
Although I have left your memory
The strength of your love teases me

I float around you in the cosmos of my spirit
You hold my delicate smile safely, in the strength of your love

DAY AND NIGHT

Each *day* you leave me
Tears roll down my heavy heart
Each *night* you leave me
It hurts me that we are so far apart

Tears fall from my eyes
As I watch the dark side of the Moon
My anticipation for your love falls from my eyes
Like the death of shooting Stars from the night skies

CRAZY FOR YOU

My heart is 'Oh so crazy for you!'
The way in which it loves you drives me wild
When you come before me, my heart speaks
You hush my lips, and I am silenced

I make a request to my heart to understand
Be calm, I say
Then when the Moon shines
My heart hurts again

In every moment of the day my heart beats so fast
In every moment of the night my heart beats so slow
My heart does not know which way to go
You hush my lips, and I am silenced forever

SPIRITUAL ATTRACTION

My spirit is attracted to your spirit
Long, hard, and deep
Without you and the Moon I cannot sleep

We have connected through our souls
But together our waters cannot flow

How can I show you my heart's desires
My heart is burning like a raging fire

HIDDEN PAIN

The way you make the world smile, with so much happiness
I see a pain that you hide
The hurt in your eyes, masked by the laughter on your lips
You show the world your happiness
Yet I see the pain you hide

The wounds that maybe time will heal
Why do you disturb those wounds of mine

If you say you love me, then give me all your pain
Take away every one of my tears
They drive me insane
My beating heart's desire is to quench my lover's pain
My beloved, take away each one of my tears again

Hide your pain in my body and love will unite us both the same

WINDING PATHS OF LOVE

The pain in my heart never gives me peace
When the soft winds blow, I think of you
And I fall like the gentle leaves

Do not cry now
You have betrayed my heart
Why hurt my heart like this
Why break my heart like this

Do not tell the world you have stolen my heart
When you have no words for me
Your arrows of rejection have struck me down
Why did I ever long for you to set my love free?

What can I say about these winding paths of love?
Who wins and who loses in this game for fools?

WANDERING MIND

Setting eyes on you is my deepest regret
Come to me my beloved, I am all cried out
Day in, day out, the thought of you agitates my mind
Without you, my mind wanders aimlessly

What is this love that strokes my soul
Setting eyes on you is my deepest regret

In my dreams I search for you
A million endeavors but you are nowhere to be seen
Come to me now my beloved
Come to me quickly as my mind will not settle

STORMS IN MY EYES

Tears are creating storms in my eyes
Pulling on my heart strings
Playing on the marks of my memories
So deep are my thoughts of you

I hold in my heart; memories of you
I become breathless
I cannot control these tears
These tears do not stop in the doorways of my eyes

Tears are creating storms in my eyes

FORGOTTEN LOVE

Oh, my dear heart, do not beat another heartbeat again
Keep all my feelings within you dear heart
Do not bring any words to my lips

Oh beloved, you remember me no more
How do I express my love now?
Tears fall from my eyes all over my soul

I gave you all my happiness and the smile on my face
The Sun and the Moon cannot be replaced
They only follow your beautiful footsteps
All love is bestowed upon you only

You spoke not a word, no goodbye
If there was ever love for me, you would not hurt me then fly
So…so far away

No one near or far can understand you dear heart
              do not beat another heartbeat again

CHANGE OF SEASONS

Every season for a reason...

Spring brings rain and new life
Summer brings sunshine and warmth
Autumn brings a soft breeze and change
Winter brings snow and peace

I have loved you through the changes of every season
I have been unloved through the changes of every season
A lonely soul yearning to sense and experience the beauty of life
Wherever beauty is seen

TELL ME YOU DON'T LOVE ME

Tell me you do not love me anymore
You cannot handle my love a single minute more
Let us both break free from the pain
So that we are free to love again

I cannot keep stopping my world for you
You invade my soul and make it bruised
I cannot keep re-opening the doors of my heart
And let you continue to shred my spirit apart

IN MY HEARTBEATS

You live in my heartbeats
My every breath says
Come to me beloved
I have lost you in my dreams

I am lost in this state of love
I long to disappear into the sky above
Come back to me forever
So, we can live and die together

You build me up
And the world continues to break me down
I am floating alone without you around
My heartbeats are slowing down now

COME TO ME

Come to me my beloved, my mind will not settle
My mind will not sleep, as I lie awake counting the stars,
I am going crazy trying to make my days pass

Searching for the Moon behind the clouds
When will I see you again?

The seasons keep on changing and still you do not come to me
In every shadow I see you
You are a shadow in my memory

When will you come to me beloved?
My mind will not settle

LOST WITHOUT YOU

Without you my heart is lost
The clouds have opened and oh so many rains have passed

Come hear my thoughts on love and pain

My body is on fire, my heart is blue
I cannot sleep without you
The night belonging to the Moon is raw
This pain of love shakes me to the core

Only God knows I have given you my heart
I cannot breathe without you
Can we go back to the start
We made promises but you have forgotten me

Oh beloved, bring me news of when we will touch
This is the burning game of love
Please do not play fire and games with my heart
Without you my heart is lost

LOST IN YOUR HEART

Nobody listens, how will they hear me?
I have lost endless nights of sleep
I am a bird without my wings
Without my beloved, what have I left in life?

My eyes will not sleep when I close them,
I am lost in my thoughts
I am lost in my pain
I am sorry for my regrets

I have lost endless nights of sleep

Sitting on my doorstep
I will wait for you forever
There are marks on the walls, and I mark the walls
I have loved and have marks on my heart

What do you take from rejecting me?
When I die, I will leave my life in your heart

WHEN YOU ARE GONE

When you are gone the bright Moon goes to sleep
The warm Sun hides behind the clouds
The shining Stars fall out of the sky
The dark nights do not pass

Without your love, my life is tasteless
The roses lose their fragrance
The days are cloudy
The birds have ended their song

Without you, life has no life left
I miss the magic in your voice
The world has become so quiet
Come home beloved soul

SAY GOODBYE

Let us say goodbye
As we erase these memories from our minds
Etched in my heart is the love of you and I
Let us pull the dark curtain over the bright blue sky

The heights of my pain throw me right back down to Earth
A love that is tainted and scarred, yet still carries its worth

A love that can never be shown must be forgotten
I will remember you in my next lifetime
        as I fall asleep on life
           my last dream will be that you return to me

This is not friendship
        this is an exchange of souls
This is not flowing water
        this is burning fire

I have signed your name in the sand
And shown time that I could be yours
But you could not show time that you could become mine
Let us put out the fire in our hearts
Let us forget each other for this lifetime

THE TIME HAS COME

The time has come
I must forget everything
I must remember nothing

Do not go so far away
That it becomes difficult for you to return
Never come so close again
That it becomes difficult for me to leave

May this yearning love never die of thirst
May the Moon in the night sky
Never be dishonoured by our love
Leave your stubbornness behind
I will leave my promises behind

Let me go
For you will never hold me in your arms
I face a lifetime of tears falling on the pages of my poetry

Your love will remain in my soul forever…

FORGOTTEN

Oh, my heart, do not beat another heartbeat again
Keep all my feelings within you dear heart
Do not bring any words to my lips

Oh, beloved you remember me no more
How can I express my love now?
Tears fall from my eyes through my soul

I gave you all my happiness and the smile on my face
The Sun and the Moon no longer come to me
They cannot be replaced
They only follow your beautiful footsteps
All love is bestowed upon you

You spoke not a word, no goodbye
If there was ever love for me, so far away you would not fly
Nobody, near or far can understand you
Dear heart do not beat heartbeats which are untrue

LOST

Please do not let me lose sight of you
I see the creation of the Universe in your eyes
I see Sunrise, Stardust, and Moonshine in disguise

I am waiting for you my soldier to rescue me
Your name is known by all

And not to mention,
This love comes from the purest of intentions
Your spirit runs through my veins
Your love is my purest pain

When I lose sight of you
My heart becomes as heavy as a Moonrock
When I see you the Sun rises again
Please do not let me lose sight of you

I see the creation of the Universe in your eyes

LOST SOUL CONNECTION

Ask the Moon to drown
Switch off the light from the Stars
Send the Sun to sleep
I have lost my soul connection
My spirit is dying
My heart and soul are fading into the Sunset
Our souls have lost connection

DO YOU THINK OF ME?

We met in a distant time
Do you think of me?

I have met you in my dreams every night
Do you think of me?

My heart is raw with pain
Do you think of me?

I will be yours forever
Do you think of me?

You are all around me
Do you think of me?

TIME SLIPS AWAY

Should our hands slip away from each other
May we never let go of our friendship
Time will never allow us to break those special moments
Your voice which my eyes await

A picture broken in a thousand pieces can never be joined
    back together
We meet little by little
Yet, I cannot even give a little of my heart to you

If a friend sits beside you, let them stay
The waters of a flowing river never flow back to you once they
    have passed

Time will never allow us to break those special moments

Separation

VI

SEPARATION

What I do not know
What I wish to know
When will I know in my heart?
Why you left and separated from me
Why have you taken that path and left me lonely again?

When will my heart understand this pain?
Why am I not loved by you?
What hurt did I cause you?

I gave my heart and soul to you
Was there ever a me and you?
Was there ever an us?

Our connection has no name
And love continues its punishing ways

I do not have a heart strong enough to continue my path alone
Tears stream down my face again
Away you have flown

What I do not know
When will I know?
Will your love ever return to me again?

IF I ASK

On every corner I see his punishment
If only he could make his life a life of love for me

He would never let me face pain
I am alone again
He has taken my pain as a souvenir of my love

If I ask, she will smile for me,
And I would steal a lie for her
If she would forget me, I would forget her not
In her love, I forget the Universe
I have fallen for her magic
Let me see the beauty of her smile on her face again

Can he put this punishment to sleep
And sweeten my smile again?

When will he give me his decision?

QUESTIONS OF LOVE

Why were you sent to me if we were not meant to be?
Why has God made a love so strong if it cannot be set free?

You keep on disappearing and then again coming back to me

When can I run into your arms?
    So you can hold me, oh so tightly
Will our souls have to wait until another time to fit together
    perfectly?

BROKEN LOVE

Time after time please do not break my heart
I wear my heart on my sleeve
You snatched my heart away and broke it all apart

The tears in my eyes have dried
I can no longer swim in the night pools of your eyes

I no longer see the Stars move and the promises in your eyes
My beloved, dark has become the night

I can console my heart no longer
I wish I would melt far away into the night sky

As our love might not get stronger
Far from the Earth and the Moon and the Stars

STRANGERS OF THE HEART

Come let us go back to the time
When we were strangers on the street
Before we met a million years ago
When you had no recollection of me

A time where I placed no hopes or desires on you
     within this heart of mine
A time where you never looked upon me
     with that lust in your eyes
A time where the beating of my heart
     never sang in every word of mine
A time when there was no poison
     in the magic of your eyes

Connecting our souls has become a burden on the heart
     and is better left forgotten
The story in which we were unknown strangers must be concluded
     as love is no longer possible

Tell me, how can we go back to a time when we were strangers?
How do I set alight fire to this beautiful love story?
The blood of my heart has poured out into the poetry of my
     words
I began making a new home of love which you will no doubt
     break in a moment

You are confused in every step you take with me
They tell me your charisma is a false trait of yours
My companionship with you will be a guilty pleasure
We must lose the nights in which you have become my protection

Let me turn and see your beauty one last time
It is time to let love go

STARVED OF A TOUCH

A deep loneliness
Tears falling in floods
A heavy heart
Hiding my sadness behind a thousand smiles
The taste of coffee on my lips

I look for things in the world to dampen my feelings and
    thoughts...

A prayer to God for strength
The comfort of a pillow for my heavy head
The softness of a towel against my skin
The warmth of the Sun in my bones
The light of the Moon and the Stars in my eyes
The longing and the hope of being held safely in his arms

One day, forever...

RAW PAIN

How will I travel this journey of life alone from today?

I feel my strong heartbeat in my eyes
   as my tears
      roll down
         they are burning my soul

My spirit dying as the Moon goes down
And the Stars fade away
Why did you build me up then throw me down?
Why do you steal my heart
And then tease it in front of the world?

Why do the spears of your rejection pierce my heart?

The Sunlight of the new day blinds me
I wish I could sleep for forever and a day
I must face the road ahead alone with a strong heart and
     invisible to all around me

The raw pain of a burn
The raw pain of a cut
Heals the pain of my soul

HOLDING ON

Is this friendship or is it love?
Is this a convenience?
Is it a rumour?
Or, is it nothing at all?

What did it mean to see love and life
In your eyes?
What did it mean to see your Stardust and Moonshine
In my life?

Because of love we have separated
Yet I am still drowned in you
Why reject this intoxication?
I am holding onto the vision of your spirit
Whilst I search for my diamond in the sky

DEATH

When I first saw you, I left my all with you
Your eyes were a whirlwind
You remain untouched on my lips

Bring back the days that have long gone
Bring back the nights that are lost

I am on the final path of my journey
I think about my dreams and wishes, my beloved
And leaving them all behind

One day our bodies will die on Earth
We shall meet again in the Universe

You take the lead, and I shall follow
We shall be King and Queen of the Universe
Floating higher, higher, higher through the Stars

UPON MY DEATH

Do not promise to see me again in this life
Our souls will not be separated by distance nor time
Your love is gentle, but stubborn you choose to be
You saved me so many times
    And I never forced you to be unhappy
I have waited so many lifetimes already

Upon my death… promise me you will come by my side
So that our souls can touch for a moment, one more time
Before I leave this Earth, I must feel your love
As the next time we meet
                we will be higher than the skies above

One day you will hold my hand
    and fly me through the Universe
When we can reach enlightenment on our special planet
    which is waiting for us

We will light up the sky
Brighter than the Sun and the Moon do
Tears of love I will cry for me and for you
As I shower my love all over you

POETRY OF OUR LOVE

To write the poetry of our love
Will take forever and a day
For two love birds to fly off into the Sunset
Will we ever have our way?

It is not each other's bodies we crave
But the love of each other's hearts and souls we long to taste

With so much distance and space between us
And the long summer hazy days
A knot has been tied in the strings of my heart
Come untie the knot so I can love freely again

Only you can heal my wounded heart
Although you have seen my deepest wounds
To kiss and heal them will take forever and a day

The journey between us seems so far
When will you hold me, touch me, and unfold me
And love me in the deepest, darkest parts of my heart

TODAY I FEEL LIKE...

I feel like crackled glass... beautiful but damaged
I feel like an eroded rock...keeping others strong but
    slowly fading away
I feel like a doormat...useful but used
I feel like an old scarf...warm but frayed at the edges

I feel like gas substance...silently floating but ready to
    explode
I feel like a wilted rose...fragrant but weak

I feel like a delicate strawberry...sweet but bitter
I want to be close to you....and kiss you deeply whilst
    I cry

BECAUSE I AM FRAGILE...

I am like glass, do not crack me
I am like a leaf, do not tear me
I am like a bracelet, do not snap me
I am like silence, come speak to my heart
I am like a snowflake, let me softly fall into your hands
I am like a bubble, come float with me
I am like a butterfly, come fly with me
I am like a spider's web, see my beauty
I am like music, come sing to me
I am like a bumble bee, come taste my honey

ONE LIFE

They say...

Life is short
You only live once
Do not live with regrets
Take the chance
If you love someone tell them
Tomorrow may never come

Yet we think...

We have all the time in the world
We will live forever
If we miss out, there will be other chances

We do not know when we will live our last day...

Fill every day with love, happiness and smiles
Do not hurt anyone
Say how you feel
Do not live in fear
Trust the truth

Our Love

VII

WHEN WILL WE MEET?

When will we meet?

When will I open my heart to you
      and share the stories of my tears?
When will I open my heart to you
      and share the stories of missing you?

When will you hold me in your arms
And feel my tears on the heartbeat of your chest?
When will we share the pain of our heartaches?

I will ask how you passed your time
Without me
Whilst I daydreamed the time away
Without you

When will we meet?
When will you hold me in your arms?
When will I open my heart to you?

LOVES ME, LOVES ME NOT

Oh, my true love
I do not wish this pain of my love on you
A broken heart that will never be fixed
A love that cannot be spoken, but is oh so true

You have turned away from my Moon, to face the Sun
I am sorry for my regrets and for my mistakes
My love for you is true
Is your love true too?

You have stolen the smile from my lips
And the laughter from my soul
Please keep them safe in your heart
Until you return them back to me

Without them I am no longer whole
Why do you silence my heart
And make my soul cry for you like this
Being in your arms is my heart's last wish

WITHOUT YOU

How do I calm my heartbeat each day?
Without you
How do I live through each day?
Without you

The Moon listens to me all through the night
As I write the poetry of our love
The Moon holds me tight through the night
And protects me from the brightness of the morning Sun

Each time I try to tell you of my love
You hush me and you silence my lips with your eyes
We can only love when we die
The night surrounds me, until that day arrives

When will my eyes find their way to you?
You had forgotten me years ago
But I still look for you each day
When will you hold me tight?
When will you fill this space inside me in every way?

My only one wish is to die before you do
So I am never lonely in this world
Without you

MY LOVE TEASE

Why do you tease me
   tease me
    tease me
     my sweet love

You tease me with your footsteps
Coming close then moving away
I hear the music of your love singing
And then my world falls silent again

Like the Sun teases the Moon
Then sets behind the evening landscape in my mind
For the sake of the Universe
The Moon waits alone in the arms of every night sky

There are words being spoken on the lips
Of the world
To one another we are silent
A love concealed between twin flames
A love that cannot be named

Do not be afraid, I am already shy
Let go of my hand, you already have all my promises
Do not be stubborn, let go of my soul if you cannot hold on
Only you give me strength and I cannot cry for you for oh so
long

Why do you tease, tease, tease my love for you?

My heart is afraid to speak
My mind will not let me sleep
My breath is thirsty for the truth
Why do I have to hide my love for you?

DREAMS

I dream of you all night
Oh, Sun do not rise in the morning
Let me dance with the Moon in its everlasting light

In daylight I cannot see you
At night I see your beauty before my eyes

The silence all around me is deafening
Bring back the sweet music into my life

LOVE POETRY

Writing the poetry of my love will take time
How do I send the messages from my body to the depths of
    his broken heart?
There is a long distance to shorten, this will take time

There is a knot that has been formed between our souls
How do I untie this knot?
Do we untie this knot to find broken strings?
A million tries to untie this knot will surely take time

He has found the deep, hidden wounds of my bleeding heart
However, these deep, scarred wounds, will take time to heal
Writing the first poetry of our love, will surely take its time

When I write the poetry of our love
 It will surely reveal my heart's desires
                and be worthy of his love and dreams
When our eyes meet, we will both find our peace
The Moonlight will shine down on us

                and smile on the poetry of our love

LOVE STORY

This love story has changed before our eyes

I have seen him change
He is for another woman
He has seen me change
I am for another man

The silver of the Moon is hidden in the clouds
How will we live our lives?
Now that this love story has changed

Destiny gives me no strength
For our love has lost its way
What was written in the Stars
Has changed its course

Before we could belong to each other
We had already parted from each other
The dreams we saw together faded into the night sky
Our happiness locked away
We had to find new hopes and dreams
Without each other

MEMORIES OF OUR LOVE

I am lost for words
    in his eyes
        in his voice

In the passion of his eyes, I saw my sweetest dreams
A stranger unknowingly bearing his soul to me

The first time I set eyes on him
I saw love on a new horizon
In a new song

Our eyes swayed and danced in and out of each other's spirits
    for not very long

I shied-away
    He also shied-away

Super Blue

Moon

VIII

MUSIC OF OUR LOVE

Oh, sweet music, play the music of our love
Let me sing his name in my poetry
Let my empty heart feel the passion of his love all around me

My lips are looking for a song to sing
So I can sing the poetry of my love, for him
Every song of him and his love
            In a concert of his love

Where there is no fear of stealing his heart
Where I can sing in ecstasy to an audience of lovers

My sweetest dreams scattered amongst the Stars
Whilst I listen out for the music of our love

LUNA GIRL

She is the Moon girl, her name is Luna
As Luna casts her dark side over the Universe
She longs to shine her Moonlight first

Luna's heart is soft and fun loving
The Earth is hard and hurts her

Luna reaches out to the Sun
And takes him on a journey through Sunset and Sunrise
Luna and the Sun are friends for life

For now, her connection with the Sun has died
And so, she closes her eyes and says goodbye

ONE DAY, FOREVER...

I am flying high through the clouds into the skies of your love
I am intoxicated by your scarred eyes
Your eyes have forced me to lose myself inside of you

Your beautiful glass eyes have pulled on my heartstrings,
    pulling me deeper into you
My foot has slipped in its step, and I have fallen right into your soul
You caught me in your arms, so I could not slip through
You wrapped the whole Universe around me, a love so true

I have fallen and cannot share
The pain of my love with a single soul
The flowers smile to soothe my tears
A long story of broken hearts, our story is old

We have hidden these shy pains from ourselves and each other
We hide so many fears
We have been protected by God, from evil eyes, for one another
So we may experience the truth of our love, for all our
    coming years

One day, forever...

SUPER BLUE MOON

Oh Beloved, tonight there is a Blue Moon
Shining in our sky
I look to the shining Moon
As I long to see you before my eyes

How many Blue Moons will pass before I see you?
I close my eyes and imagine you holding me close to you
Just once in this Blue Moon...

I surrender myself to the Blue Moon
I desire you for me
        as I am only for you
Every step I take in life, I will pray for you
        in the light of this Blue Moon and always

Oh, Blue Moon, do not hide your bright side behind the grey clouds
In the same way that I hide my love and light
Come let us shine our love together on this night, so loud
Oh Moon, we only have each other on this dark night

Blue Moon, fill the void of our love
I may not be on this Earth to see him before you next return
Shine all your colours onto me
For the Sun has deceived me

Oh beloved, you are so deep within my deepest thoughts
You are in my heart, spirit, and soul

My twin flame, my soulmate, my yearning nirvana
My one love, my pure love, my true love

Printed in Great Britain
by Amazon